Michael Lang

IT Architecture and Risk Management

Fundamentals - Methodology - Techniques - Critical assessn

Michael Lang

IT Architecture and Risk Management

Fundamentals - Methodology - Techniques - Critical assessment

GRIN Verlag

Bibliografische Information der Deutschen Nationalbibliothek: Die Deutsche Bibliothek
verzeichnet diese Publikation in der Deutschen Nationalbibliografie; detaillierte bibliografische Daten sind im Internet über http://dnb.d-nb.de/ abrufbar.

1. Auflage 2011
Copyright © 2011 GRIN Verlag
http://www.grin.com/
Druck und Bindung: Books on Demand GmbH, Norderstedt Germany
ISBN 978-3-640-91608-5

IT Architecture and Risk Management

Fundamentals - Methodology - Techniques - Critical assessment

Assignment
in the Module

Enterprise and IT Architecture Management
at the
AKAD Privat-Hochschulen

created by
Michael Lang

Neu-Ulm, April 2011

Declaration of Authorship

Hereby I declare that I have written this assignment with the title

IT Architecture and Risk Management

by my own. Furthermore, I confirm that no other sources have been used than those specified in the assignment itself. This assignment, in same or similar form, has not been available to any audit authority yet.

24th of April 2011

Michael Lang

Contents

List of Figures

List of Abbreviations

AA   Application Architecture

COBIT   Control Objectives for Information Technology

COSO   Committee of Sponsoring Organization of the Treadway Commission

FMEA   Failure of Mode Effects Analysis

ICT   Information and Communication Technology

IEC   International Electrotechnical for Commission

IEEE   Institute of Electrical and Electronics Engineers

ISO   International Organization for Standardization

IT   Information Technology

KPI   Key Performance Indicator

NIST   National Institute of Standards and Technology

PIM   Plattform-Independent Model

PMI   Project Management Institute

PSM   Plattform-Specific Model

SA   Systems Architecture

SEC   United States Security and Exchange Commission

SWOT   Strength Weakness Opportunities Threats

TOGAF   The Open Group Architecture Framework

USA   United States of America

Chapter 1

Introduction

"In the twenty-first century, IT architecture will be the determining factor.

The factor that separates the winners from the losers, the successful and the failures, the survivors from the others."

(Zachman, 1996, p. 2)

The author Zachman (1996, p. 7) emphasises in his article the growing significance of *IT architecture* for modern enterprises. According to Zachman (1996, p. 1) *IT architecture* aligns business strategy with information technology and enables the achievement of business goals. Therefore, an efficient *IT architecture* is a key factor for companies which are faced with increasing changing markets and shorter product life cycles. In contrast to that, an estimated 68% of corporate IT projects are neither on time nor on budget and they don't deliver the original stated business goals (Jeffery & Leliveld, 2004). Regarding Fairbanks (2010, p. 8) a major cause for this is an insufficient *risk management* in the *IT architecture* development in principle. Therefore many *IT architects* ask themselves, how they could identify and prioritize their project's most pressing risks? Which architecture and design techniques mitigate the risks and what is the amount of risk reduction?

In order to answer these questions, section 2.1 defines the terms *architecture* and *enterprise architecture* before it deals with the *IT architecture* itself. The following section 2.2 gives an overview of *risk* and *risk management* in general.

Chapter 3 presents the main chapter of this assignment. At first, it gives a brief overview of the role of *IT risk management* in the scope of strategic management. The next two sections illustrate the *IT risk management* and *IT risk management process*. In addition to that, section 3.4 describes different instruments for *IT risk analysis* whereas section 3.5 shows how *IT risk management* can be implemented in the *architecture life cycle*. The section 3.6 outlines the regulations which affect *IT risk management*.

Moreover chapter 4 discusses the benefits and limitations of *IT risk management*. Finally chapter 5 summarizes the basic insights and gives a short perspective.

Chapter 2

Fundamentals

2.1 Fundamentals of Enterprise and IT Architecture

2.1.1 Architecture

In reference to Lankhorst (2009, p. 1) *architecture* helps to manage the complexity of any large organisation, software or system with a blueprint and general principles. Therefore, the term *architecture* can be defined as the following:

"Architecture is the fundamental organization of a system embodied in its components, their relationships to each other and to the environment and the principles guiding its design and evolution." (IEEE, 2000)

2.1.2 Enterprise Architecture

Definition of Enterprise Architecture

Regarding Keller (2006, p. 14) an *architecture* at the level of an entire organisation is commonly defined as *enterprise architecture (EA)*. In contrast to the general definition of *architecture*, *enterprise architecture* is settled at a higher level. It has a less technical and more business oriented focus (Keller, 2006, p. 15). This leads us to the following definition of *enterprise architecture*:

"A coherent whole of principles methods and models that are used in the design and realisation of an enterprises organizational structure, business processes, information systems, and infrastructure." (Lankhorst, 2009, p.3)

Basic Structure of Enterprise Architecture

In general, the basic structure of an *EA* can be represented by three main levels, called *business, application* and *system architecture* (Niemann, 2010). The main levels with their components are shown in the *EA pyramid* and will be shortly characterised (Figure 2.1):

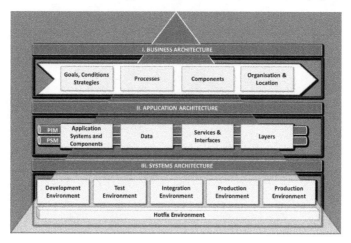

Figure 2.1: EA Pyramid (Niemann, 2006, p. 17, adjusted diagram)

1. **Business Architecture** is a collection of plans, that describe the major business of an enterprise (Niemann, 2010, p. 86). The parts of *business architecture* are goals, conditions, components, organisations and business processes. The following two layers concentrate on the alignment of the business processes in order to fulfill an optimal *IT* support.

2. **Application Architecture** provides a blueprint of the entire *application systems* and *services* with the corresponding technologies. It clarifies the interaction between the enterprise's systems and the their relationships to the business processes (Keller, 2006, p. 30).

3. **System Architecture** specifies the *physical landscape* of an enterprise. On the one side, it describes the physical deployment of every *application system*. On the other side it gives an overall view of the configuration of communication networks, servers and low-level software components.

Benefits of Enterprise Architecture

The benefits of *EA* can be separated into three main groups:

- **IT Efficiency:** *EA* defines a set of guidelines, best practices and standards. This leads to do things right at a higher level.

- **IT Effectiveness:** *EA* provides a knowledge base and support for decision making. Thus, it helps to select the right things.

- **IT Reliability:** *EA* represents a transparent view of the whole enterprise. Therefore, risks can be recognized and eliminated in an early stage.

2.1.3 IT Architecture and Architecture Management

Definition of IT Architecture

Regarding Niemann (2006, p. 21) *IT architecture* represents a blueprint for enterprise *IT systems*. Therefore, *IT architecture* comprises the layers *application architecture* and *system architecture* of the *EA pyramid* (Engels, 2008, p. 78). Its counterpart is *business architecture* which is already defined as a layer in the *EA pyramid* (Figure 2.2).

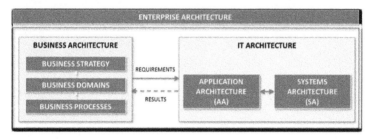

Figure 2.2: IT Architecture - Element of Enterprise Architecture (Engels, 2008, p. 78)

Architecture Management

Architecture management is related to Niemann (2006, p. 22) a continuous process of aligning *IT architecture* at *business core processes*. According to the *Deming cycle*, the primary functions of *IT architecture management* are *documenting, analysing, planning, acting* and *checking* (Figure B.1).

2.2 Risk and Risk Management

2.2.1 Risk

Risk is defined as the product of the *likelihood* of an event and its *impact* (Kouns & Minoli, 2010, p. 34). Therefore, it can be expressed in the following mathematical formula:

$$Risk = (Probability\ of\ event\ occurring) \times (Impact\ of\ event\ occurring)$$

Probability: It is a measure of how likely will a particular event occur.

Impact: The expected value of the loss.

The formula points out, that less probable events with a high impact have the same *risk* like events with a higher probability but low impact. The left diagrams gives an overview of the overall *risk components* (Figure 2.3).

2.2.2 Risk Management

In reference to Kerzner (2009, p. 746) *risk management* can be summarized as follows:

- **Definition:** *Risk management* is the practice of dealing with risk. It includes *planning* for risks, *identifying* risks, *analysing* risks, development of *risk response* strategies and at last *monitoring* and *controlling* risks in order to determine how they have changed (Figure 2.3) (Kerzner, 2009, p. 746).

- **Objective:** The major objective of *risk management* is to avoid or mitigate the probability and impact of negative events (PMI, 2008, p. 273).

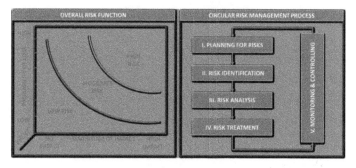

Figure 2.3: Elements of Risk and Risk Management (Kerzner, 2009, pp. 744-746)

Chapter 3

IT Risk Management

3.1 Role of IT Risk Management

In order to understand the important role of *IT risk management* for *IT architecture*, the methodology has to be arranged in the area of *strategic management* (Figure 3.1):

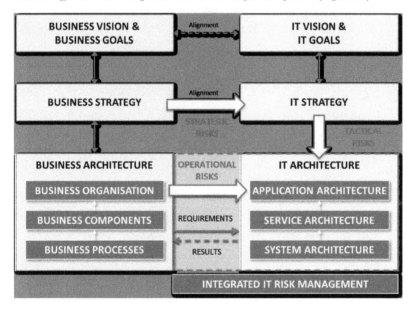

Figure 3.1: Role of IT Risk Management (Hofmann & Schmidt, 2007, p. 72)

1. **Business and IT Goals:** A *business goal* is derived from a *business vision*. It defines a long-term aspiration of an enterprise in the future. An *IT goal* is also derived from a *IT vision*. Moreover, it shall also be aligned at the *business goals*.

2. **Business and IT-Strategy:** The *business* and *IT strategy* determine how the *business* and *IT goals* shall be achieved.

3. **Business and IT Architecture:** The *business* and *IT architecture* represent the *enterprise architecture*. The *business architecture* is responsible for the *business processes* whereas the *IT architecture* looks for the optimal *IT support* (Hofmann & Schmidt, 2007, p. 72.)

In this context, *IT architects* are faced with *strategic, tactical* and *operational IT risks*. For this reason, they need an effective management process for dealing with them. Thus, the next three sections show, how a concrete *IT risk management process* looks like and what are the best instruments. Section 3.5 illustrates how *IT risk management* can be implemented in the whole *architecture management process*.

3.2 IT Risk Management

In general, *IT risk management* deals with all areas of *risks* which are related to *IT*. Regarding Hofmann & Schmidt (2007, p. 72) *IT risks* can be separated in three main groups (Figure 3.2):

The benefits of *EA* can be separated into three main groups:

- **IT Strategic Risks** cover all *IT risks* within the strategic context. A possible *IT risk* can be an insufficient coordination between *business* and *IT strategy*.

- **IT Tactical Risks** describe the level of risks between strategic and operational level. A wrong decision of an enterprise application is an example for this area. The enterprise application can not be adjusted according the changed legislation.

- **IT Operational Risks** are the day-to-day risks for an *IT architect*. For instance, this contains security, performance and availability risks of the *IT architecture*.

Figure 3.2: Groups of IT Risk (own diagram)

3.3 IT Risk Management Process

The following *IT risk management process* is based on the *ISO/IEC 27005* standard (ISO & IEC, 2008). The process consists of several steps and can be implemented in every *IT architecture project* (Figure 3.3):

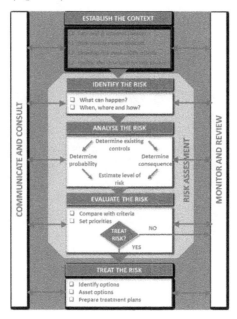

Figure 3.3: IT Risk Management Process (Königs, 2009, p. 32)

Step 1 - Communication and Consult

Communication and consultation aims to identify who should be involved in an *risk assessment* for a concrete *IT architecture project.*

Step 2 - Establish Context

This step contains the definition of a strategy and methods for identifying and analysing *risks.* This contains of a *risk management plan* and a *risk register* for gathering *risks* (PMI, 2008, p. 282).

Step 3 - Identify Risks

The aim of this step is to identify possible risks that may affect the *IT architecture* in a negative way (Kerzner, 2009, p. 755). The *risks* can be collected through *brain storming*, *interviews* or *SWOT analysis* by answering the following questions: *What can happen, how can it happen* and *why could it happen?*

Step 4 - Analyse Risks

The next step is to classify *risks* with respect to their *impact* and *probability*. A *risk classification scheme* can looks like follows (The Open Group, 2009) (Figure 3.4):

EFFECT	FREQUENCY				
	FREQUENT	LIKELY	OCCASIONAL	SELDOM	UNELIKELY
CATASTROPHIC	Extreme	Extreme	High	High	Moderate
CRITICAL	Extreme	High	High	Moderate	Low
MARGINAL	High	Moderate	Moderate	Low	Low
NEGLIGIBLE	Moderate	Low	Low	Low	Low

Figure 3.4: IT Risk Classification Scheme (The Open Group, 2009, p. 350)

Step 5 - Evaluate Risks

After the classification of the *IT risks* the *It architecture group* decides in this step whether *risks* are acceptable or need treatment. The result of the *risk evaluation* is a prioritised list of *risks* that require further action (Kerzner, 2009, p. 761).

Step 6 - Treat Risks

This step is responsible for developing options to reduce *risks* of an *IT architecture*. Regarding Kerzner (2009, p. 782) there exists four typical strategies for *risk treatment*:

- **Risk Avoidance** involves changing the former *IT architecture plan* in order to eliminate the *risk* entirely.

- **Risk Transfer** requires shifting the negative impact of a *risk* to a third party. This action does not eliminate the *risk*.

- **Risk Mitigation** implies the reduction in the *probability* and/or *impact* of a *risk*.

- **Risk Acceptance** indicates that the *architecture team* plans to deal with the *risk* or is unable to identify any other suitable response strategy.

Step 7 - Monitor and Review Risks

The *IT architect* must monitor periodically *risks* to ensure that the *risk register* is up-to-date. Besides, the effectiveness of the *risk treatment* must be reviewed continuously.

A few risks will remain static. Therefore the *IT risk management process* needs to be regularly repeated, so that new *risks* are captured in the process and effectively managed.

3.4 IT Risk Analysis Instruments

This section gives an overview of different *instruments* for the determination of *risk values* in the context of *IT risk analysis*. These *instruments* can be used for the evaluation of the whole *IT architecture*, a *IT project* or a single *IT system* (Königs, 2009) (Figure 3.5):

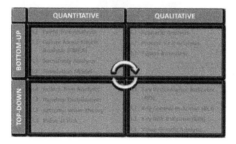

Figure 3.5: Risk Analysis Methods (Königs, 2009, p. 43)

In principle, the *analysis instruments* will be divided into *bottom-up* and *top-down analysis*. Moreover, the *analysis* will be separated if they provide *qualitative* or *quantitative* results:

- **Bottom-Up Analysis** is an inductive approach. It identifies and quantifies possible negative events following an initiating cause. In this context, the *risks* of an *IT architecture* would be evaluated with the analysis of its sub-systems. An example for this approach is the *event tree analysis* (Figure C.1)

- **Top-Down Analysis** use a deductive approach. It defines top negative events and then use backward logic to define possible causes. These top negative events represent identified hazards or system failure modes. An example for the *top-down analysis* is the *Value Benefit Analysis* (Figure C.2)

3.5 IT Risk Management in Architecture Life Cycle

Regarding NIST (2002, p. 4) an effective *risk management* has to be totally integrated into the *architecture life cycles* of an enterprise. For instance, the life cycle of an *IT system* contains of five phases (Figure 3.5). In this context, *IT risk management* is an iterative process that can be performed during each phase of the *system life cycle* (Table B.2).

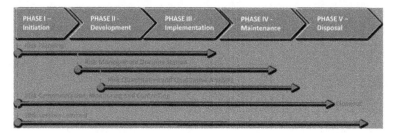

Figure 3.6: IT Risk Management in Architecture Life Cycle (NIST, 2002, p. 5)

3.6 IT Risk Management and Compliance

The last years are marked with violation and *miss management* in enterprises (Königs, 2009, p. 64). Therefore, new regulations have been adopted which shall lead to a transparent *risk management* in enterprises. This section gives a short overview of regulations which affects also the *IT risk management* of enterprises:

- **KonTraG:** The *KonTraG* is operative in germany since 1998. It demands a companywide *risk management* in corporations. In relation to *IT risk management* it requests mainly an adequate *IT security management* (Hofmann & Schmidt, 2007)

- **Sarban-Oklay Act and COBIT:** The *Sarban-Oxley Act (SOX)* was passed in the USA in 2002. It demands companies to introduce an adequate *Internal Control Structure* like the *COSO* framework by the *SEC*. The *IT* control framework *COBIT* is often used for the fulfillment of *SOX* in the *IT* sector (Königs, 2009, p. 76).

Chapter 4

Discussion

The previous chapter dealt with the role and application of *risk management* in the field of *IT Architecture*. The following section discusses the fundamental benefits and limitations of *IT risk management*.

4.1 Benefits of IT Risk Management

1. **Risks promotion:** The key element of *IT risk management* is the promotion of risks to prominence. This leads to that all stakeholders accept and understand the necessity of dealing with those risks. The result is the reduction of operational surprises and losses. *IT architects* gain enhanced capability to identify potential events and establish responses, reducing surprises and associated costs or losses (Fairbanks, 2011, p. 8).

2. **Systematic approach:** On the on side, *IT risk management* is a systematic approach, which helps *IT architects* to deal with risks in a correct manner. On the other side, it is also a collection of best practices for analysing exposure to risk, measuring or assessing risk and then developing strategies to mitigate risks. The result is a risk treatment at an early project state (COSO, 2004, p. 1).

3. **Enhancing risk response decisions:** *IT risk management* provides the strength to identify and select among alternative risk responses like risk avoidance, reduction, sharing and acceptance (Kerzner, 2009, p. 782).

4. **Identifying and managing multiple IT risks:** Every enterprise faces a myriad of risks affecting different parts of the *IT architecture*. An *IT risk management* facilitates effective response to the correlated impacts (COSO, 2004, p. 1).

5. **Improving deployment of capital:** A robust risk information allows *IT architects* to effectively assess overall capital needs and enhance capital allocation.

6. **Simple and clear presentation:** The *risk analysis instruments* like the *IT risk classification scheme* compares possible events on usually two main assessment criterias. Through this focused presentation, *IT risks* can be prioritised and corresponding *risk treatments* can be easier selected (The Open Group, 2009, p. 350).

7. **Improving communication between IT and management:** *IT architects* can justify their *IT demands* objectively with a risk register instead of simply request them. On the other side, *IT risk management* helps the business to understand the impact of each *IT project* on the whole enterprise architecture. This leads to a better communication between management and *IT architects* (Fairbanks, 2011, p. 8).

4.2 Limitations of IT Risk Management

1. **Misusage of IT risk management:** Regarding Power (2007) *risk management* can be misused for the handling of uncertainty. In general, *risk management systems* are often applied to transform complex and ambiguous situations into seemingly comprehensible risks. This leads to the idea that all risks can be managed. This is an illusion. Therefore, an *IT architect* has to understand that with an *IT risk management* he can only handle risks, which are in the scope of his responsibility.

2. **No decision making:** *IT risk management* will not make the decisions for the *IT architects*. It can only assist an *IT architecture* owner in making decisions. However, the decisions will be limited by the depth of the research and analysis of risk. Besides, the decisions are also limited by the experience of the decision makers and by people not being involved in the decision making process.

3. **Limited guarantee:** It is impossible to be able to predict all negative consequences of an *IT architecture* decision. Where humans are involved there is always the possibility that a mistake may happen that will lead to an incident. Therefore, *IT risk management* can help to be prepared for an adverse consequence in a limited way.

4. **Not fail-safe:** The *IT risk analysis* should attempt to identify all significant risk but it will be limited by the resources available, including information at hand, involvement of stakeholders, time and budget. On the whole, *IT risk management* does not actually remove the risk. It just reduces the negative effects when bad things happen.

Chapter 5

Summary and Prospects

The introduction of *IT risk management* in the *IT architecture process* provides a decisive input for the realisation of *IT strategies*. An effective *IT risk management* helps to identify and prioritize *IT risks*. In order to understand the importance of *IT risk management*, section 2.1 gave an introduction in *enterprise* and *IT architecture* before it deals with the *risk* and *risk management* itself.

Chapter 3.1 gave in its first section a brief overview of the role of *IT risk management* in *enterprise*. The sections 3.2 and 3.3 dealed with the term *IT risk management* in detail and shows how a concrete *IT risk management process* looks like. Moreover, section 3.4 gave an overview of different *instruments* for the *IT risk analysis* whereas section 3.5 outlines how *IT risk management* can be integrated into the *IT architecture life cycle*. Section 3.6 listed important enterprise regulations which affect also the *IT risk management*. Chapter 4 discussed the benefits and limits of *IT risk management*. On the one side, *IT risk managements* helps to identify significant risks at an early phase. On the other side, critics argue that *IT risk management* can only assist *IT architects* in making decisions in a limited way. In the end, decisions are carried by humans.

Despite the weakness, *IT risk management* helps *IT architects* to be prepared for adverse consequences and mitigates negative surprises. In contrast to that, in next years enterprises will continue to intensify the use of third party *IT services* and reduce internal legacy production. Though *IT services* can almost completely be taken over external service providers, the associated risk can not. Therefore, *IT risk management* will play a more and more important role for enterprises in a globalized world.

Pohlmann summarises:

"IT risks are business risks. Those risks can not be outsourced."

(Pohlmann, Reimer & Schneider, 2011)

15

Bibliography

[1]   COSO (2004). *Enterprise Risk Management - Integrated Framework.*
       Retrieved April 20, 2011, from http://www.coso.org.

[2]   Engels, G. (2008). *Quasar Enterprise: Anwendungslandschaften serviceorientiert
       gestalten* (1st ed.). Heidelberg, Germany: dpunkt Verlag.

[3]   Fairbanks, G. (2010). *Just Enough Software Architecture: A Risk-Driven Approach*
       (1st ed.). Boulder, CO: Marshall & Brainerd.

[4]   Fairbanks, G. (2011). Just Enough Architecture: The Risk-Driven Model. *Cross
       Talk, 23* (6), 8-11.

[5]   Gadatsch, A., & Mayer, E. (2006). *Masterkurs IT-Controlling* (3rd ed.).
       Wiesbaden, Germany: Vieweg Verlag.

[6]   Hofmann, J., & Schmidt, W. (2007). *Masterkurs IT-Management* (1st ed.).
       Wiesbaden, Germany: Vieweg Verlag.

[7]   IEEE (2000). *IEEE Std 1471-2000: Recommended Practice for Architectural
       Description of Software-Intensive Systems.* Piscataway, NJ: IEEE Computer
       Society.

[8]   ISO, & IEC (2008). *ISO/IEC 27005:2008 information security standard.*
       Geneva, Switzerland: International Organization for Standardization (ISO).

[9]   Jeffery, M., & Leliveld, I. (2004). *Best Practices in IT Portfolio Management,*
       Retrieved   April   20,   2011,   from   http://sloanreview.
       mit.edu/the-magazine/articles/2004/spring/45309/
       best-practices-in-it-portfolio-management.

[10]   Keller, W. (2006). *IT-Unternehmensarchitektur: Von der Geschäftsstrategie zur
       optimalen IT-Unterstützung* (1st ed.). Heidelberg, Germany: dpunkt Verlag.

[11]   Kerzner, H. (2009). *Project Management: A Systems Approach to Planning,
       Scheduling, and Controlling* (10th ed.). Hoboken, NJ: John Wiley & Sons.

[12]   Königs, H.-P. (2009). *IT-Risiko-Management mit System* (3rd ed.).
        Wiesbaden, Germany: Vieweg+Teubner Verlag.

[13]   Kouns, J., & Minoli, D. (2010). *Information Security Risk Management* (1st ed.).
        Hoboken, NJ: John Wiley & Sons.

[14]   Lankhorst, M. (2009). *Enterprise Architecture at Work: Modelling, Communication and Analysis* (2nd ed.). Heidelberg, Germany: Springer Verlag.

[15]   Ludewig, J., & Lichter, H. (2010). *Software Engineering: Grundlagen, Menschen, Prozesse, Techniken* (2nd ed.). Heidelberg, Germany: dpunkt Verlag.

[16]   Niemann, K. D. (2006). *From Enterprise Architecture to IT Governance* (1st ed.).
        Wiesbaden, Germany: Vieweg Verlag.

[17]   NIST (2002). *Risk Management Guide for Information Technology Systems* (9th ed.). Gaithersburg, MD: National Institute of Standards and Technology.

[18]   Pohlmann, N., Reimer, H., & Schneider, W. (2011). *ISSE 2010 Securing Electronic Business Processes* (1st ed.). Wiesbaden, Germany: Vieweg+Teubner Verlag.

[19]   Power, M. (2007). *Organized Uncertainty: Designing a World of Risk Management.* Oxford, United Kingdom: Oxford University Press.

[20]   Project Management Institute (2008). *A Guide to the Project Management Body of Knowledge* (4th ed.). Newtown Square, PA: Project Management Institute.

[21]   The Open Group (2009). *The Open Group Architecture Framework (TOGAF)* (9th ed.). San Francisco, CA: The Open Group.

[22]   Zachman, J. (1996). *Enterprise Architecture: The Issue of the Century.*
        Retrieved April 18, 2011, from http://www.zifa.com.

Appendix A

Enterprise Architecture

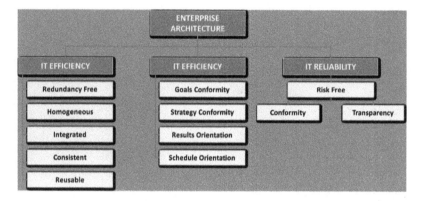

Figure A.1: Benefits of Enterprise Architecture (Niemann, 2006, p. 46)

Appendix B

IT Architecture

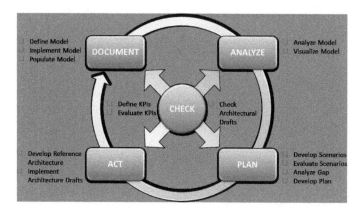

Figure B.1: IT Architecture Development Cycle (Niemann, 2006, p. 73, adjusted diagram)

IT SYSTEM LIFE CYCLE	PHASE CHARACTERISTICS	SUPPORT OF IT RISK MANAGEMENT
Phase I - **Initiation**	❏ Need of an IT system is expressed ❏ Purpose and scope are documented	❏ Risk identification in order to support the system requirements ❏ Support in development security concept
Phase II - **Development**	❏ Design of IT system ❏ Development, and purchase of IT system components	❏ Support security analysis ❏ Support design trade-offs ❏ Support product trade-offs
Phase III - **Implementation**	❏ IT system security features are configured, tested and verified	❏ supports the assessment of the system against the requirements
Phase IV - **Maintenance**	❏ System performs its function ❏ Modifications in hardware and software are made through process, policies or organisational changes	❏ Risk management activities are performed for reauthorization or reaccreditation
Phase V - **Disposal**	❏ disposition of information, hardware, and software ❏ Sanitizing the hardware and software	❏ Risk management activities are performed for system components that will be disposed of or replaced ❏ System migration is conducted in a secure and systematic manner

Figure B.2: IT Risk Management in System Life Cycle (NIST, 2002, p. 5)

Appendix C

IT Risk Analysis Instruments

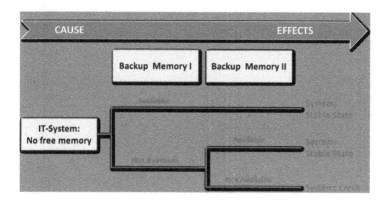

Figure C.1: Event Tree Analysis (own diagram)

	IT Systems				
ATTRIBUTES	WEIGHT	IT-SYSTEM A	TOTAL A	IT-SYSTEM B	TOTAL B
USABILITY	20	3	60	5	100
MAINTAINABILITY	30	2	60	3	90
RELIABILITY	50	1	50	3	150
TOTAL	100		170		340
RANK			2		1
Scale: 0 – 5, (0 = not existing 5 = excellent)					

Figure C.2: Value Benefit Analysis of IT Systems (Gadatsch & Mayer, 2006, p. 221)